I0045435

AN IDEAS INTO ACTION GUIDEBOOK

Critical Reflections

How Groups Can Learn from Success and Failure

IDEAS INTO ACTION GUIDEBOOKS

Aimed at managers and executives who are concerned with their own and others' development, each guidebook in this series gives specific advice on how to complete a developmental task or solve a leadership problem.

LEAD CONTRIBUTORS	Chris Ernst
	André Martin
CONTRIBUTORS	Joan Gurvis
	Kelly Hannum
	Michael Hoppe
	Richard Hughes
	Cynthia D. McCauley
	Chuck Palus
DIRECTOR OF PUBLICATIONS	Martin Wilcox
EDITOR	Peter Scisco
ASSOCIATE EDITOR	Karen Mayworth
WRITER	Selby Bateman
DESIGN AND LAYOUT	Joanne Ferguson
CONTRIBUTING ARTISTS	Laura J. Gibson
	Chris Wilson, 29 & Company

CCL No. 429
ISBN-10: 1-882197-93-3
ISBN-13: 978-1-882197-93-4

CENTER FOR CREATIVE LEADERSHIP
WWW.CCL.ORG

Critical Reflections

How Groups Can Learn from Success and Failure

Chris Ernst and André Martin

Center for
Creative
Leadership®

THE IDEAS INTO ACTION GUIDEBOOK SERIES

This series of guidebooks draws on the practical knowledge that the Center for Creative Leadership (CCL®) has generated, since its inception in 1970, through its research and educational activity conducted in partnership with hundreds of thousands of managers and executives. Much of this knowledge is shared—in a way that is distinct from the typical university department, professional association, or consultancy. CCL is not simply a collection of individual experts, although the individual credentials of its staff are impressive; rather it is a community, with its members holding certain principles in common and working together to understand and generate practical responses to today's leadership and organizational challenges.

The purpose of the series is to provide managers with specific advice on how to complete a developmental task or solve a leadership challenge. In doing that, the series carries out CCL's mission to advance the understanding, practice, and development of leadership for the benefit of society worldwide. We think you will find the Ideas Into Action Guidebooks an important addition to your leadership toolkit.

Table of Contents

EXECUTIVE BRIEF

Critical Reflections is a process that leaders can use to help their groups learn lessons from key events, positive or negative. The basic process is short and simple. It begins with a key event and includes three stages: exploring—reliving the event and sharing perceptions of what happened; reflecting—reaching an understanding of how and why it happened; and projecting—harvesting lessons for the future. The goal is to create a specific action plan that will set the stage for a productive future.

Leading with Critical Reflections

In a world of complexity and rapid change, one certainty is that individuals, groups, and organizations that can continually learn from experience will be more flexible at meeting the challenges of tomorrow. When people undertake shared work over time, certain key events stand out as having the potential to teach lasting lessons to the group as a whole. These types of experiences are the classrooms in which people learn, improve, and grow.

Yet these lessons of experience can easily be missed in the pursuit of the next big project, client, or initiative. To capture the best repeatable practices and identify avoidable mistakes, groups need to be able to learn in the moment, as they work, not afterward when it's too late to change.

Group leaders play an important role in this process. As a leader, have you ever

- been part of a project that never felt complete—in which, somehow, things were left unsaid or tasks left undone?

- found yourself halfway into an initiative when you suddenly had a feeling of déjà-vu but couldn't pinpoint what you had learned the last time around?

- felt you let an opportunity float by—an opportunity to capture meaningful learning for yourself, your group, or your organization as a whole?

- been part of an event or initiative and felt frustrated that the lessons experienced by the group could not be transferred and shared with the organization as a whole?

Critical Reflections will help you address all of these kinds of situations. Unlike away-from-work training or conferences, the learning that takes place from Critical Reflections happens on the job. The process embeds learning into doing the work itself, helping you simultaneously achieve organizational results and new learning and growth.

First Things First

Before you begin the Critical Reflections process with your group, you as the leader need to identify the key event, allocate time and space, and prepare to orient your group.

Identify the Key Event

You may find that this first step takes care of itself. Something strikingly good—or bad—may happen within your group that clearly holds lessons for the future. Be alert to such opportunities. Whether the key event was a great success or a wretched failure, your goal will be to affect future outcomes in similar situations. Key events could include any of the following:

- Crisis situation
- Important meeting
- Change in the group members
- Change in the leadership of a group
- Achieving an important milestone
- Completing a change initiative
- Hitting or missing a financial target
- End of a quarter

See the sidebar on the next page for a couple of examples.

Key Events: Positive and Negative

The senior management team of a regional hospital was working to create a more collaborative culture and to become a more customer-focused hospital. The hospital's CEO, a classic type A manager, was trying to change in his relationship with his team to create more of an environment of shared leadership, shared ownership, shared accountability, and shared learning. Over a period of several quarters, the team made significant headway in trying to practice a more inclusive leadership model.

In the midst of that process, the hospital found itself in a crisis situation, dealing with a massive overflow of patients from a large explosion at a local construction site. The hospital responded with high levels of professionalism: communication flowed quickly and openly, hospital units coordinated activities to allow for a quick response to emerging needs, and the staff displayed selfless dedication and commitment. The staff's performance and positive patient-confidence reports following the explosion seemed to show that the hospital was on the right track.

Then the team members were presented with data from the next quarterly survey and discovered that there had been a huge dip in patient confidence. They were stunned. One member asked, "Why haven't we been able to create consistency in patient confidence?" Things fell apart, and the team members reverted to old behaviors. The CEO dominated the discussion, the directors of the various functional units pointed fingers at one another's departments, and open communication collapsed.

This meeting was a key event for the hospital team. How could the team move forward from this collapse, learning not only what had just occurred but also how to avoid such events in the future? The hospital team could also use Critical Reflections to learn valuable lessons from its initial great success in dealing with the overflow of patients from the explosion. Successful leaders and their groups learn from such key events—both positive and negative. That is the goal of the Critical Reflections process: to help leaders and their groups learn lessons of experience and, ultimately, share what they've learned with their organizations.

Allocate Time and Space

After a key event has occurred and you have decided to use the Critical Reflections process, set aside some time and secure a space for your group to use. Depending on the importance of the key event and the complexity of the situation, Critical Reflections can be as quick as a process check at the end of a meeting or as extensive as a half-day session. Your commitment to the investment of time, whether short or long, sends a message to your group that this is an important part of its work, not an extra thing to worry about. The reflection should be done in a group of about four to twenty people. It should take place shortly after the key event to ensure that feelings, thoughts, and actions are fresh on everyone's mind.

Prepare to Orient Your Group

Your next step is to prepare to give your group an overview of the Critical Reflections process. You should be able to answer the following questions for your group.

1. **Why are we here?** Our objective is to reflect on the key event in order to pull out lessons of experience that we can take forward.

2. **What are we going to do today?** We will put the key event "in the middle"; in other words, we will reflect on it and learn from it by thinking of it as an object that we can discuss fully in a nonthreatening and enlightening way. To do this, we will work through the three stages of the Critical Reflections process: exploring, reflecting, and projecting.

3. **Why is this process important?** The exploring stage will help us relive the event and share our individual

perceptions of what actually happened. The reflecting stage will help us reach an understanding of how and why it happened. The projecting stage will help us harvest lessons for the future: what we should keep doing, what we should stop doing, and what we should do differently.

4. **What is your role in the process?** Your role is to participate in the dialogue.

5. **What are the ground rules for behavior?** If differences surface among us, we will keep them in the middle—that place where we can reflect on them and learn from them. By depersonalizing the event in this way, we can all participate without feeling threatened.

These questions and their answers help to keep you and your group on track as you go through the stages of the Critical Reflections process. When your group has had some experience with the process, a brief reminder of this overview is probably all that will be needed.

Finally, you need to formulate a framing question before calling your group together. This question should be clear and concise, focused on the key event, and nonjudgmental. It serves to focus the attention of the group on a single compelling and thought-provoking issue. It helps to frame the discussion and related activities. The following are examples:

- What is the most pressing challenge that our group currently faces?

- Where are we falling short in the execution of our strategy?

- How did the key event impact our work? What happened as a result?

- What can we learn from achieving (or not achieving) our strategic objective?

Framing questions are similar to "powerful questions." The information on pages 14–15 may be helpful to you in creating framing questions.

The Basic Process

The Critical Reflections process is used with groups to capture lessons of experience, from both successful and unsuccessful events. The process allows groups to take a key event and figuratively place it in the middle—that is, as an object on which to reflect and from which to learn. The concept of putting something in the middle permits groups to suspend judgment and to focus their attention in a constructive and positive way.

The process begins with a key event and moves through three stages:

- exploring—reliving the event and sharing perceptions of what happened
- reflecting—reaching an understanding of how and why it happened
- projecting—harvesting lessons for the future

This section provides a brief overview of the entire process so that you can begin using it right away. The following section offers some advanced options that you may find helpful when you're familiar and comfortable with the basic process.

Exploring

In this stage, the goal is to put the individuals and the group as a whole back in the moment of the key event. Ask each member of your group what—from his or her own perspective—actually happened. What was the sequence of events? What were they thinking? What were they feeling? What did they do? Get each person's viewpoint on how it was back then when it happened. The purpose is to allow them to relive the event—to share perceptions, to appreciate differences, to identify overlaps and disconnects of personal experiences.

Reflecting

Now interpret the event. What assumptions were operating? What were instances of cause and effect? How was it possible for the event to happen, and why did it? The reflecting stage of the process uncovers obstacles, highlights key actions, and sheds light on hidden beliefs.

A Shared Reality?

The overarching outcome of Critical Reflections is learning from experience. Some lessons of experience will be shared; others will be unique to the individual. In a similar way, sometimes a shared reality will emerge, and other times not. Each step of the Critical Reflections process creates the conditions for, and can move a group closer to, a shared reality, but this would not be necessary for the process to be effective. Even realizing that your perception of reality is not shared by others is a very worthwhile lesson of experience.

Asking Powerful Questions

Powerful questions are aimed at the root of issues facing leaders and their organizations—the values, assumptions, perceptions, and emotions that can form a wedge between a challenge and a solution. By asking powerful questions, leaders are able to uncover aspects of a challenge that might have been ignored or overlooked in the past, called negative space. There are three characteristics that typically distinguish powerful questions: they invite exploration, resist easy answers, and invoke strong passions. In essence, powerful questions affect the way we gather information by helping us move beyond simple intellectual analysis to create a more holistic view of the challenge. What follows is a description of several types of powerful questions, along with examples of each type.

R-mode questions (so named because they are associated with the right hemisphere of the brain) promote patterns, synthesis, visual metaphors, emotions, or intuitions:

- What are the patterns?

- What is interesting or unique about this challenge?

- What is one hope you have regarding this challenge? What is one fear?

- How do you feel about this challenge? What is your intuition saying?

Imagination questions pose surprising scenarios and encourage imaginative thinking:

- What if we deliberately tried to make this challenge worse?

14

- What would happen if we threw everything away and started over?
- What would our "blue sky" solution look like?

Wild-card questions focus on scenarios that are highly unlikely or stretch our sense of reality:

- What are the most important wild cards for my organization, my customers, and me?
- What would wipe our organization out or make us obsolete?
- What are three future trends that could totally change the way we do business?

So-what questions get at the underlying values of an individual or group:

- What is the value we are unwilling to give up?
- What are we trying to achieve? What purpose does our mission serve?
- What's so important about this challenge?
- What's so great about our solution?

Positive-frame questions focus on what is going right through appreciative inquiry:

- What are we doing right?
- What are our strengths?
- To what do we aspire?

Projecting

Based on the group members' understanding of what happened and how and why it happened, then so what? What lessons can be learned? What should they keep doing, what should they stop doing, and what should they do differently? What do they need to do either to repeat the current success or to avoid making the same mistake again? These lessons can be at the individual, group, or organizational level and can relate to either relationships or the task itself. The goal is to plan the next steps—to create a specific action plan that will set the stage for a productive future. Make sure there is accountability for each of the steps. Write the plan and revisit it at the next meeting.

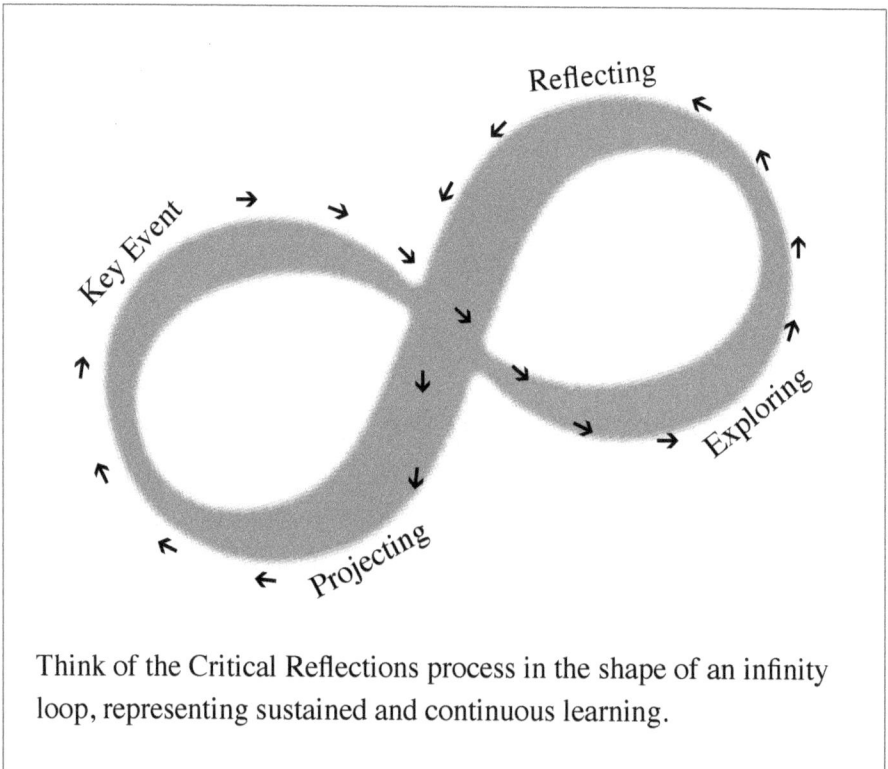

Think of the Critical Reflections process in the shape of an infinity loop, representing sustained and continuous learning.

Advanced Options

The basic Critical Reflections process is short and simple: exploring, reflecting, projecting. As with learning almost any other process, it's good to begin with the basics, repeat them, and master them. After you've done that, you may want to consider some more advanced options. What follows is a description of some of the activities that can be used in more extensive versions of the Critical Reflections process.

Activities for Exploring

The following activities are useful in the exploring stage of the process.

Personal story writing. The purpose of this personalizing activity is to get group members to show candor about their individual perceptions of the key event. In this activity, each member of the group is asked to write a short story that represents his or her individual experience of the key event.

Story-Writing Ground Rules

1. Start by thinking about the question and then begin writing. Write anything that comes to mind, without judging your writing. Just keep your hand moving.

2. Write down words, images you see in your mind. Take one word and write it down. Write all your thoughts and meanings around it.

3. Trust yourself; don't try too hard. Let it flow and, again, don't judge while you are writing.

The story should include answers to these five questions:

- Where was I when the event occurred?
- How did I feel about the event?
- What did I think about the event?
- How did I react in response to the event?
- What did I personally lose or gain as a result of the event?

Story writing is a personal, reflective exercise, and—if the key event was negative—it can bring pain, discomfort, and even embarrassment for some individuals. In leading your group members through this activity, stress that they are not obligated to share their stories. The stories frequently are useful when dealing with difficult topics, and they require a certain degree of candor from group members. Guaranteeing anonymity and confidentiality opens the door to the candor the group needs at this point.

CCL's experience shows how liberating and even cathartic this activity can be when group members know in advance that it is a safe, private process. It may be the first time that they have allowed themselves to think openly about the event, particularly if it was a negative experience. It can prepare group members for moving from a private, guarded understanding to a public space from which they can draw shared lessons.

Creating Endings

This is a good follow-up activity to use with personal story writing. Place the group members in a circle and invite them to share one emotion, thought, or reaction they are letting go of to allow the group to move forward. Then have them throw their stories away.

Collage. The purpose of this imaging activity is to allow each member to better understand the perspectives of the others in the room. In this activity, each group member is asked to select an image to put in the middle. These images can come from all kinds of sources, including old magazines, printed artworks, postcards, and so on. It is important to have a broad and varied selection of images to accommodate the many possible perspectives of group members. Members of the group are asked to select pictures that speak to them about how they felt during the event. Instead of or in addition to a picture, group members can employ famous quotations or actual objects. Any of these mementos can help group members reveal to themselves and to one another how they view the earlier experience.

For example, one member might choose a photo of the earth from outer space, showing a large hurricane with its spiraling, all-encompassing chaos. Another member might choose a photo of a kayaker navigating through turbulent white-water rapids. Such images are powerful and evocative; they have the capacity to open understanding so that people can see things they have not seen before. They can inspire free-flowing discussion about the key event, giving your group members an opportunity and a process to talk about it freely. You may feel the energy level rising in the room, with healthy laughter and a sharing of perspectives around the images that are chosen.

CCL's Visual Explorer is a tool developed to facilitate such discussions. It includes more than two hundred color images that invite examination and explication, and it is therefore a useful resource for groups seeking to explore complex topics. For more information, see page 26.

Activities for Reflecting

The following activities are useful in the reflecting stage of the process.

Affinity mapping. The purpose of this mapping activity is to analyze the key event step by step and to uncover what went well, what went wrong, and what the group's guiding assumptions were. To begin the activity, identify at least three periods of time in the event, which could be as simple as beginning, middle, and end. Group members can use different colors of large sticky notes to place up on a wall or boards to represent what went well, what the major obstacles or challenges were, and what the individual assumptions were. If your organization has access to groupware, such as some kind of digital whiteboard, your group can use that instead of sticky notes. More important than the type of technology is your group's focusing on the task at hand and the relationships.

Gallery walk. This theming activity works well after the mapping activity above. Its purpose is to uncover themes and patterns in the individuals' responses during the mapping activity. In this activity, the group members interact with the affinity map by reading the responses, grouping them by theme, and adding new ideas if desired. This process of identifying themes may uncover deep unspoken feelings and truths, competing commitments, and differing perceptions and assumptions. The goal is for your group to use these themes and patterns as a springboard to the lessons in the next stage of the Critical Reflections process.

Activities for Projecting

The following activities are useful in the projecting stage of the process.

Reframing. The purpose of this activity is to allow the group to reframe what occurred during the key event in the context of their new understandings. In this activity, your group uses the themes that emerged from the affinity maps to reframe the key event and pull out lessons of experience. Each member is asked to identify and share something that he or she has learned that can be taken away as a lesson from the day's activities. Give each person the opportunity to suggest ground rules, group processes, and work procedures that should be implemented to make sure that the lessons learned will be incorporated into the work of the group. Then choose the new behaviors that the group can commit to moving forward. It is important to focus on no more than five to seven new behaviors to ensure that the group will not be overwhelmed.

A Second Chance

If the key event was a meeting, the group actually has the opportunity for a "do-over," a chance to relive the same event with new learning and a more positive outcome.

Journey map. The purpose of this crafting activity is to create a single story that will serve as a guide for your group and as a way for your group to communicate what it has learned to other individuals, groups, and the organization as a whole. Ask your group members to work together to write a story that includes these five parts:

- Call to adventure—What was the event or challenge that faced the group?
- Creating a fellowship—What did you do or not do to build strong commitment?

- Discovering gifts—What did you learn as a result of facing the challenge?

- Tipping point—What were the three biggest obstacles you had to overcome?

- Journey home—What actionable advice (tangible processes, tools, tips, norms) could you give other groups in the organization?

This step not only helps your group capture its unique experience but also creates a road map for other groups in the organization as they try to achieve their own goals.

Other Activities

Personal story writing, collage, affinity mapping, gallery walk, reframing, and journey map are good tools to have in your Critical Reflections toolbox. But they are by no means the only possibilities. The Critical Reflections process is structured powerfully but flexibly, allowing a leader to work with a group in ways that will fit the particular organization and event. You or your organization may have your own tools to draw on that will also work well in the process.

Leadership and Organizational Learning

When groups and organizations undertake shared work over time, certain key events often stand out—events that leave a lasting impression on the group. The unique depth, breadth, and intensity of these events provide a dramatic test of the leadership strategies of the group. New strategies may be developed, old strategies may be reverted to, or current and established strategies may be employed.

Unfortunately, groups and organizations often neglect the powerful opportunity for learning that accompanies a key event. At best, an after-action review may be conducted to capture technical issues. The relational and social issues so pivotal to the effective handling of a complex challenge are often not dealt with.

Critical Reflections allows groups and organizations to more fully understand the impact of the key event on their leadership strategies and to project forward in order to incorporate the learning from the event into future interactions. By implementing Critical Reflections in your own leadership, team-building, and continuous learning strategies, you give yourself, your group, and your entire organization a powerful way to make continuous learning concurrent with the continuous work that must go on.

Suggested Readings

Dixon, N. M. (1996). *Perspectives on dialogue: Making talk developmental for individuals and organizations.* Greensboro, NC: Center for Creative Leadership.

Drath, W. H. (2001). *The deep blue sea: Rethinking the source of leadership.* San Francisco: Jossey-Bass.

Palus, C. J., & Horth, D. M. (2002). *The leader's edge: Six creative competencies for navigating complex challenges.* San Francisco: Jossey-Bass.

Raymond, C. C., Eichinger, R. W., & Lombardo, M. M. (2001–2004). *FYI for teams.* Minneapolis, MN: Lominger Limited, Inc.

Yamashita, K., & Spataro, S. (2004). *Unstuck: A tool for yourself, your team, and your world.* New York: Portfolio.

Background

The Center for Creative Leadership works with many organizations and teams to help them develop team management skills through experience with practical team-oriented applications. These developmental experiences provide research-based information about how high-performance teams work and proven approaches for turning average performers into a highly effective team. Through training programs, research, and custom interventions, CCL continues to provide a hands-on learning experience for leaders that emphasizes a range of practical tools and strategies for enhancing the performance of any group.

As a part of this overarching approach, Critical Reflections assists groups and organizations in making the implicit leadership strategies adopted during a key event explicit. Through principles of storytelling and dialogue, assumptions are surfaced and perspectives shared across boundaries, which in turn allows for the development of connections between groups and organizations.

Key Point Summary

When people undertake shared work over time, certain key events stand out as having the potential to teach lasting lessons. To capture the best repeatable practices and identify avoidable mistakes, groups need to be able to learn as they work. Critical Reflections helps you simultaneously achieve organizational results and new learning and growth.

Before calling your group together for the Critical Reflections process, you as the leader need to identify the key event (positive or negative), allocate time and space for the process, and prepare to orient your group.

The basic process includes three stages: exploring, reflecting, and projecting. In the exploring stage, the goal is to allow your group members to relive the event—to share perceptions, to appreciate differences, to identify overlaps and disconnects of personal experiences. The reflecting stage provides the opportunity to interpret the event. How was it possible for the event to happen, and why did it? Then, based on the group's understanding of what happened and how and why it happened, move into the projecting stage. What lessons can be learned? What should your group members keep doing, what should they stop doing, and what should they do differently? What do they need to do either to repeat the current success or to avoid making the same mistake again?

When you're familiar and comfortable with the basics, you may want to consider a more extensive version of the process. Advanced options include personal story writing and collage for the exploring stage, affinity mapping and gallery walk for the reflecting stage, and reframing and journey map for the projecting stage. You or your organization may also have tools of your own that will work well in the process.

By implementing the Critical Reflections process, you give yourself, your group, and your entire organization a powerful way to make continuous learning concurrent with the continuous work that must go on.

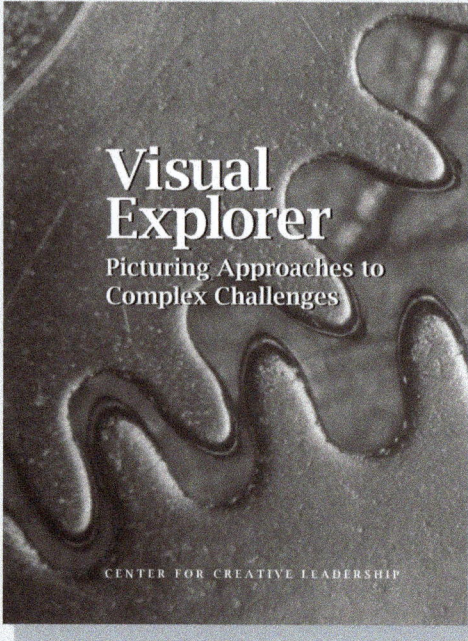

INTRODUCING A RESOURCE FROM CCL PRESS that can open new doors for learning and discovery in organizations. Put research into action using interactive development opportunities that can be facilitated without special training.

Visual Explorer
Picturing Approaches to Complex Challenges

Visual Explorer facilitates dialogue and helps groups reach a shared understanding about specific challenges. It includes a facilitator guide and 224 carefully chosen color images that invite examination and explication, and thereby acts as a resource for groups seeking to explore complex topics. Groups using Visual Explorer can collectively explore a complex topic from a variety of perspectives, building a shared understanding for making choices and taking action. (A Visual Explorer session occurs under the guidance of a facilitator.)

Stock No. 723. To get more information or to order, go to **www.ccl. org/publications**.

Related Publications

HOW TO FORM A TEAM: FIVE KEYS TO HIGH PERFORMANCE

If you are a department head or project manager, or if you are the senior-level champion or sponsor of a proposed team, you need to understand the five factors critical to building effective teams and how to use those factors to lay the groundwork for successful teams. (Stock No. 414)

HOW TO LAUNCH A TEAM: START RIGHT FOR SUCCESS

Getting your team off on the right foot is critical to its success. To launch a team so that it increases its chance of success, managers and team leaders should pay attention to four critical points: setting purpose and direction, defining roles and responsibilities, designing procedures and practices, and building cooperation and relationships. Understanding and implementing these elements is key to helping your team accomplish its mission. (Stock No. 417)

LEADING DISPERSED TEAMS

Dispersed teams are a necessary, strategic work unit in a world that continues to grow more interconnected every day. Guiding them to their full potential is a difficult challenge for even the most seasoned team leader. Solving potential communication problems and devising processes for making decisions and managing conflict are key leadership challenges for those managers. Creating an effective first-time meeting and securing organizational support are critical to success. (Stock No. 423)

MAINTAINING TEAM PERFORMANCE

Team success isn't inevitable. Leaders who monitor and maintain their team so that it operates at peak efficiency can ensure that it successfully achieves its goal. By assessing their team's effort, knowledge and skills, tactics, and group dynamics, leaders can diagnose problems and make corrections to bring the team back on track. (Stock No. 420)

RAISING SENSITIVE ISSUES IN A TEAM

Have you ever wondered how to deal with a sensitive issue within your team? For example, how do you raise the issue that the women rarely get listened to? How do you bring up your observation that the team members from Marketing always dominate the meetings? This guidebook focuses on ways to determine whether to raise such an issue in a team meeting—and if so, how. (Stock No. 437)

Purchase our **TEAMS GUIDEBOOK PACKAGE** (Stock No. 732) and receive the above five titles at a significant savings. See below for ordering information.

Ordering Information

TO GET MORE INFORMATION, TO ORDER OTHER IDEAS INTO ACTION GUIDEBOOKS, OR TO FIND OUT ABOUT BULK-ORDER DISCOUNTS, PLEASE CONTACT US BY PHONE AT 336-545-2810 OR VISIT OUR ONLINE BOOKSTORE AT WWW.CCL. ORG/GUIDEBOOKS.

www.ingramcontent.com/pod-product-compliance
Lightning Source LLC
Chambersburg PA
CBHW042119190326
41519CB00030B/7553